We Go to School

Sharon Coan, M.S.Ed.

then

now

then

now

then

now

then

8

now

then

now

then

now

then

now

then

now

Write It!

1. Think about schools then.
2. Think about schools now.

3. Draw a picture of a school then.

4. Draw a picture of a school now.

Glossary

now—at the present time

then—in the past

Index

Your Turn!

How have schools changed? How are they the same? Tell about it.